WILLIAM WALTON

TWO PIECES FOR VIOLIN AND PIANO

EDITED BY
HUGH MACDONALD

PIANO

MUSIC DEPARTMENT

OXFORD
UNIVERSITY PRESS

to Vivien and Larry

Two Pieces
for Violin and Piano

I
Canzonetta

WILLIAM WALTON

*Based on a troubadour melody.

OXFORD UNIVERSITY PRESS, MUSIC DEPARTMENT, GREAT CLARENDON STREET, OXFORD OX2 6DP

4

II
Scherzetto

WILLIAM WALTON

TWO PIECES FOR VIOLIN AND PIANO

EDITED BY
HUGH MACDONALD

VIOLIN

MUSIC DEPARTMENT

OXFORD
UNIVERSITY PRESS

OXFORD
UNIVERSITY PRESS

Great Clarendon Street, Oxford OX2 6DP, England
198 Madison Avenue, New York, NY 10016, USA

Oxford University Press is a department of the University of Oxford.
It furthers the University's aim of excellence in research, scholarship,
and education by publishing worldwide in

Oxford New York

Auckland Cape Town Hong Kong Karachi
Kuala Lumpur Madrid Melbourne Mexico City Nairobi
New Delhi Shanghai Taipei Toronto

With offices in

Argentina Austria Brazil Chile Czech Republic France Greece
Guatemala Hungary Italy Japan Poland Portugal Singapore
South Korea Switzerland Thailand Turkey Ukraine Vietnam

Oxford is a registered trade mark of Oxford University Press
in the UK and in certain other countries

© Oxford University Press 1951, 2008, 2009

Database right Oxford University Press (maker)

First published 1951
New edition published 2008
This score and part published 2009

ISBN 978–0–19–336616–9

Music origination by Enigma Music Production Services, Amersham, Bucks.
Printed in Great Britain on acid-free paper by
Caligraving Ltd., Thetford, Norfolk

TWO PIECES FOR VIOLIN AND PIANO

Two pieces
for Violin and Piano

WILLIAM WALTON

I
Canzonetta

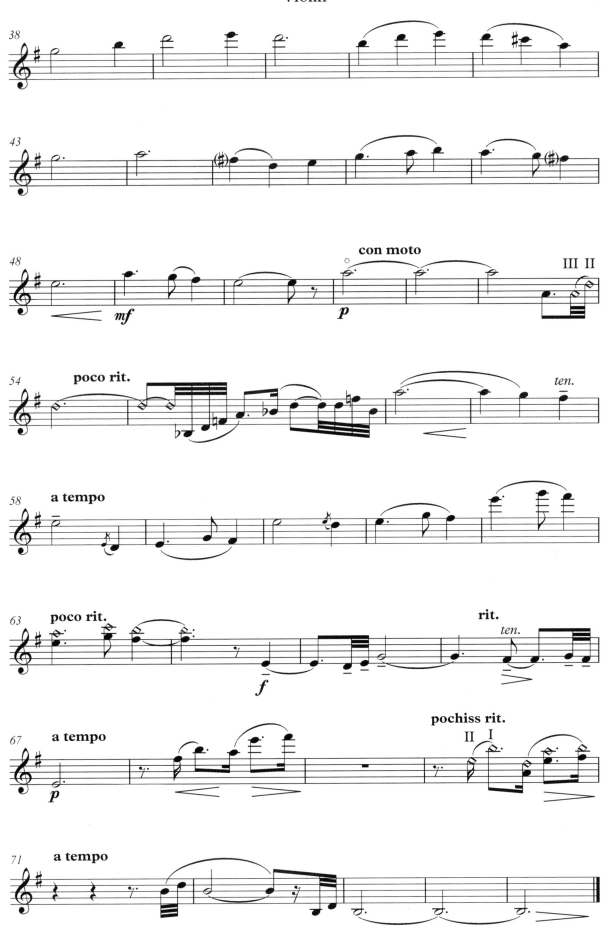

II
Scherzetto

Molto vivace